GO FOR THE FLAG

TOM WEISKOPF

GO for the FLAG.

The Fundamentals of Golf

PHOTOGRAPHS BY
KARL RAUSCHKOLB

HAWTHORN BOOKS, INC.
Publishers/NEW YORK
A Howard & Wyndham Company

Library of Congress Catalog Card Number: 78-80280
ISBN: 0-8015-3018-0

5 6 7 8 9 10

AUTHOR'S NOTE

THE AUTHOR wishes to thank Tom Place, golf editor of the Cleveland *Plain Dealer,* whose assistance in the organizing and writing of GO FOR THE FLAG has been extensive and invaluable. The author would also like to thank Karl Rauschkolb for his fine photographs specially taken to illustrate this edition. Thanks are due also to my many friends and associates who have helped in the preparation of this book.

Tom Weiskopf

ALL OF THE MEN who played golf under Bob Kepler at Ohio State University knew him affectionately as the "old coach." Many have gone on to fine careers with the help he passed along.

The "old coach" was my guiding light at OSU. He still gives me advice when I have a problem with my golf game.

For his efforts in helping me to become a better golf professional, I dedicate this book to him.

Tom Weiskopf

CONTENTS

Introduction 3

1. The Mental Side of Golf 5

2. The Clubs to Use 10

3. Putting: The Grip 12

4. Putting: Choose Your Grip 14

5. Putting: Stance 16

6. Putting: Three Ways to Do It 18

7. Putting: Slow and Easy 20

8. Putting: Always Practice 22

9. Loosen Up a Little 24

10. Start with the Feet 26

11. Posture Is the Secret 28

12. Look in the Mirror 30

13. Check Your Posture Again 32

14. The All-Important Grip 34

15. Try Overlapping 36

16. Test Them All 38

17. Step into the Shot 40

18. Find the Ball 42

19. The Big Swing 44

20. "Slide" into the Ball 46

21. Chipping Off the Strokes 48

22. Choke Down on Chips 50

23. And Now Pitching 52

24. The Pitching Wedge 54

25. The Short Irons 56

26. The Middle Irons 58

27. The Long Irons 60

28. The Fairway Woods 62

29. The Rough's Tough 64

30. The Hills and Dales 66

31. Don't Fall Over 68

32. Follow the Slope Down 70

33. Follow the Slope Up 72

34. The Good Sand Lie 74

35. The Sand Will Help You 76

36. The Buried Sand Lie 78

37. Dig the Ball Out 80

38. Everyone Needs Practice 82

39. Keep Your Clubs Shining 84

40. Know the Rules 86

    Epilogue 88

GO FOR THE FLAG

INTRODUCTION

IT REALLY WASN'T so long ago when Mom and Dad gave me my first set of golf clubs. I was fourteen years old and starting my freshman year at Benedictine High School in Cleveland, Ohio. The summer before, I had had my first taste of golf when I caddied at two country clubs near my home in Bedford, a suburb of Cleveland. Right away, I knew this was the game for me. Fortunately, my parents could understand this desire. They were excellent golfers when they were young—and they still play well.

The first time I played eighteen holes, I shot a 92. Within two months, the score was down to the high 70s. The next year, as a sophomore in high school, I made the varsity golf team.

All of this may sound as if golf came easily. In a way I suppose it did, but few people knew of the many hours I practiced. After school, every day, my parents could find me on the high school football field, hitting golf balls until dark.

During this time I never had a formal, complete lesson. That didn't come until I went to Ohio State University. Bob Kepler, the golf coach at OSU at the time, did more for my game than anyone else. He taught me the fine points of golf. I had figured out many of the shots by myself, simply by observing others and experimenting. But Coach Kepler put the finishing touches on the shots. He started to give my game the polish it needed.

There have been many others who have gone out of their way to be helpful. Jack Nicklaus was—and still is—a great inspiration to me. We were at Ohio State at the same time, although

Jack was a few years ahead of me. Jack helped then and he helps now when I ask. He has given me valuable advice on such things as attitude and course management, which means knowing how to play certain courses.

Tommy Bolt is another. A former United States Open champion, he always has been regarded as one of the finest shotmakers in the game. On the professional tour there are many times we must play shots that the average golfer never sees or thinks about. Tommy spent countless hours talking to me about these.

I could go on and on naming the people who have been helpful. They include a number of the touring professionals whom I regard as close friends. We help each other, talking about everything from how to play shots to attitude.

One person who has played an extremely important role in my rise toward the top has been my wife, Jeanne. She has thrilled at the fine rounds and suffered through the bad. She's always there, with a word of encouragement.

There were times when I wondered what I had to do to win my first major professional championship. It came in February, 1968, when I eagled the final hole to win the Andy Williams-San Diego Open. It had to be one of the happiest moments of my life.

Later that year, in July, I came from behind in the final round of the Buick Open at Flint, Michigan, to win my second championship. Now I knew I had arrived as a top-flight professional golfer.

Because many, many people have helped me, I now want to try to help others. That is why I decided to write this book for young people who are learning to enjoy this wonderful game.

The lessons on the following pages are my own ideas and those that have been taught to me.

I am not saying this is the only way to play the game. I am hopeful, though, that within these pages you will find the information that will help you to become a better golfer.

Tom Weiskopf

4

1 THE MENTAL SIDE OF GOLF

BEN HOGAN has said the one thing that makes golf such a wonderful game is that "no one ever has conquered it, and no one ever will." This is quite a statement coming from the man many believe is the greatest player in the history of golf.

It makes you realize the challenge the game presents. It is this challenge that pulls millions of boys and girls, men and women, onto golf courses every year.

The challenges are present on every hole. They are the same for every golfer, from the leading professional to the teen-ager playing for the first time. This is what helps to make golf so enjoyable for everyone.

On the following pages I am going to explain to you, in words and pictures, how to build a sounder golf game. You must know the fundamentals, such as how to take a proper stance, how to grip the clubs, and how to take a nice, smooth swing.

But there is more to winning and enjoying golf than mastering the techniques. Such things as attitude and etiquette are also important. I can speak on these subjects because attitude and temperament have played an important part in my rise to championships.

Even before I begin to show you how to hold a golf club, there are a few things you should know and remember.

ATTITUDE

NEVER BECOME DISCOURAGED, even on those days when you might not be playing as well as you should. Even the greatest of the professionals has a bad day.

Watch others, especially the better players. Say to yourself, "If he can do it, so can I."

Don't be afraid to ask questions if there is something you don't understand.

Try to get along with everyone. Make friends and help each other.

If a friend is able to use a No. 7 iron on a hole, don't feel discouraged if you can't hit the ball as far and must use a No. 5 iron, for example. As long as you can get your par, just as he does, then you are as good as he is.

Never get so mad that you throw a club. Remember, how you act reflects how mature you are.

Be humble. No matter how good you may be now, sooner or later you will find yourself meeting someone who plays better.

Don't laugh at a playing partner who is having trouble hitting his shots. Instead, encourage him.

The important thing is never to give up. If you have tried, there is no reason to be sad if you have not scored well. Play the game all the way to the final hole. Every champion has to overcome the bad days.

ETIQUETTE

A GOLF COURSE is a beautiful piece of landscape. Never do anything to mar it.

Always replace your divots.

6

If you have been in a sand trap, rake it smooth when you are finished. You wouldn't want to have your golf ball roll into a deep footprint that someone else neglected to smooth out.

If you have lost a golf ball and must spend time looking for it, let the group behind you play through. Don't hold up everyone on the course.

Learn to play fast, by not lingering between shots. You always can slow down if it becomes necessary.

You don't have to rush the actual shots. Take your time on these, but once you make a decision, play it. The professionals say, "Study a shot long, and you'll study it wrong." The first decision usually is the right one.

Be a good sport, win or lose.

Whatever you do, don't cheat. If you hit a ball in the rough, play it from the rough. Always mark down the right score, regardless of what it might be.

Make it a point to know at least a few of the basic rules of golf, as written by the United States Golf Association. They are designed to help you.

PREPARING FOR THE GAME

SOME PEOPLE, when they see the professionals in brightly colored clothes, get the idea that all they have to do is dress the same way to become a winner. You know this isn't true.

To begin with, let me say that if you can't afford a pair of golf shoes with spikes, then wear tennis shoes. They will work just as well.

As for a glove, I'd suggest you learn to play without one. This will help you to obtain a better feel for the club. If you develop a firm grip without the glove, you will be a better player.

How about a hat? I'd suggest you wear one of some sort, especially in hot weather. It will save a few sunburned noses and help to keep the glare of the sun from your eyes.

As for sunglasses, it isn't a good idea to wear them when you play, unless they have been prescribed by your doctor. It is more difficult to judge distances with them. That is why there only are two or three professionals on the tour who wear them, and they have been prescribed.

Regarding golf balls, you should use one of standard compression. Never try to hit one of 90 or 100 compression. These balls are only for the very strong players. Your home pro can help you select the proper balls.

When I started, I would play with golf balls that might be slightly scarred. I know you can't afford new golf balls all the time, but you will play better with one that is perfect. You can keep the cut and scarred balls to use when you are practicing.

THE GAME ITSELF

EVERYONE SHOULD LEARN the fundamentals of golf as soon as they begin to play the game. This book tells you the most important things to remember.

If you have a chance, let a professional in your area help you. He can get you started on the right foot. When you are young, though, I don't believe you should go through long, formal lesson periods. I never had a golf lesson until I went to college. I don't believe boys and girls are able to move into the advance stages of golf until they are at least sixteen years old.

After you have been given the basics, find out for yourself what you can do. You are in a period when you will be growing fast. Your strength and temperament will change. When I was graduated from high school, I was only five-feet, nine-inches tall. But I grew six inches in one year, and at the end of my freshman year at Ohio State University, I was six-feet-three, my present height.

Check out the fundamentals and execute them over and over again until you become a champion.

I know this system works, because I used it myself.

As you read through the instructions on the following pages, you will notice that I have started with the putter. This is because putting is the portion of your game where you can save the greatest number of strokes.

Then we will discuss the basics of the other parts of the game, such as the stance and grip, and go on to the movements of the big swing. Finally, we will discuss the way to hit the various clubs, starting with the short irons and moving into the woods.

I have followed this order because this is a book of the fundamentals. When you see a professional practice, he will start with the short irons and work his way back to the driver. He gradually builds up to the big swing. This, I believe, is the way you should learn to play the wonderful game of golf.

2 THE CLUBS TO USE

THE ACCOMPANYING PHOTOGRAPH shows the clubs I use. The set includes a driver and a No. 3 wood; a No. 1 through No. 9 iron, along with a pitching wedge, sand wedge, and putter.

Starting on the left, notice the gradual difference in the loft of the club face as you go from the driver to the sand wedge. The putter is on the right end.

If you cannot afford the complete set, I'd advise you to get a No. 2 wood and a No. 4 wood; the No. 3, 5, 7, and 9 irons; a wedge and a putter.

I recommend the two wood instead of the driver. You will find it easier to get the ball airborne with this club. It will help your confidence, and there really won't be much difference in the distance. I used a two wood until I was a senior in high school.

The shaft in the clubs is most important. Never use the stiff shaft—the regular will give you the best results now. The length will be determined by your height. A golf professional at a club in your area can tell you what is best for you.

Regarding the grip, you should make sure you can hold the club securely. If you have large hands, you may need oversize

grips. The reverse is true for those with small hands. Again, consult the club professional for his advice on this.

3 PUTTING: The Grip

THERE IS A DIFFERENCE between the grip used on the putter and the grip used on all the other clubs.

While putting, you should hold the club more in the palms of your hands and *not* the fingers. Both the *back* of the left hand and the *palm* of the right hand should face the hole, as illustrated in the first picture.

The "V" formed by the thumbs on the grip should point straight up the arms, as illustrated by the arrows in the second picture. Also note the position of the thumbs. They are placed on *top* of the shaft, pointing down the shaft. The hands are more to the side of the club rather than toward the top. This helps to eliminate the wrist break.

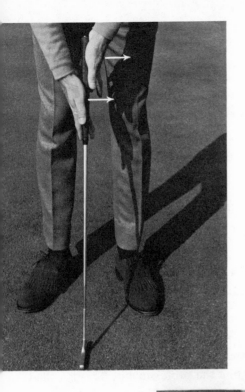

4 PUTTING: Choose Your Grip

HERE IS ANOTHER VIEW of the grip that I use and the one that is generally most popular among the professionals. This is called the "reverse overlap." Notice how the forefinger of my left hand rests on the small finger of the right hand.

This is a good grip, but it doesn't mean it is perfect for everyone. When you watch the pros, you will see many different putting styles. Choose one that feels comfortable to you. You could use the baseball-type grip, but the palms of your hands still should hold the club. This is important.

You will notice I am not wearing a glove. I do wear a glove for all the other shots. If you do wear a glove, you will have a better "feel" of the club if you take it off before you putt. Again, try it and see what is best for you.

5 PUTTING: Stance

NOW YOU ARE READY to stand over the ball. You will notice I play the ball more off the left side.

Always use a square stance, with the toes pointing straight forward. The toes are square, too. A line drawn across the front of each foot would be parallel to the line of the putt. This helps to keep the putt on a truer line.

As you address the ball, your hands should be even with the ball, not ahead or behind.

Your elbows should be in close to your body. This helps with the control of the stroke.

Try different stances. See how far apart you like your feet. Position the ball in two or three different places, such as closer to the left foot and also farther back than I have it here. See what feels best for you.

6 PUTTING: Three Ways to Do It

THERE ARE THREE BASIC WAYS TO PUTT—wrist putting, arm and shoulder with no wrist putting, and a combination.

Wrist putting is when you move the putter by bending your wrists.

Arm and shoulder with no wrists means you keep your wrists stiff, and swing the club with an arm and shoulder movement.

The combination uses the best features of both.

Again, try them all and see what is best for you. No one can tell you how to putt—this is a matter of feel. By practicing, you will learn which method is best for you.

In all putting, the left hand dominates. It keeps the putter in the intended line. Let it do the work.

7 PUTTING: Slow and Easy

WHEN YOU FEEL COMFORTABLE OVER THE BALL, you are ready to send it running for the cup.

Take the putter back slow and easy. I can't stress that enough —*slow* and *easy*.

Notice in this sequence how I take the putter straight back

from the ball. When I follow through, the blade of the putter still is following the ball right toward the target, low to the ground. You always accelerate the putter *through* the ball.

Keep your eyes down. Don't lift your head or shoulders, until you complete the stroke. Your back should be rigid throughout.

Take it from me, the good putters *hear* the tricky short putts go in, they don't see them. They keep their head down. If you move too soon, you might have a tendency to pull the putter out of line.

Listen for the "Plunk!" It's the sweetest sound in golf, as the ball drops into the bottom of the cup.

8 PUTTING: Always Practice

IT IS AS IMPORTANT TO PRACTICE with the putter as it is to practice with the other clubs. Don't make the mistake, as so many people do, of practicing on the long putts all the time. Move in close to the hole, and work on the three-, four-, and five-footers. They are the ones that will make the biggest difference in your score.

If you had one hundred long putts, chances are you would make only a few, if any. Even when you chip and run, you will be putting the ball close to the hole. That means you will have many short ones to make. If you don't have the touch for those, you could miss them, too.

22

9 LOOSEN UP A LITTLE

BEFORE YOU HIT the first golf ball for the day, take a few moments to stretch your muscles. This is especially important if you do not have time to hit several practice shots.

One of the best methods is to take two or three of your irons and swing them. The girls may find it easier to swing one or two clubs. It will help to loosen arm, back, and hip muscles.

You certainly do not want to feel stiff or rigid on the first tee. This will help that situation. Also, you might place a club across your back, hold it with the inside of your elbows as a brace, and turn several times at the waist, to the right and then the left.

The more relaxed you can be when you prepare for the first shot, the better it will be for you. A good drive off the first tee is the first step to an enjoyable round of golf.

10 START WITH THE FEET

THERE ARE THREE BASIC TYPES OF STANCES—the open, as shown in the top picture; the square, as in the middle picture; and the closed, as in the bottom picture. The golf club in front of my feet is used to illustrate the direction of the target area.

In all three cases my right foot is pointing straight ahead or perpendicular to the line of flight. The left foot is pointed slightly toward the target (approximately thirty degrees).

The open stance basically is for the short irons, the chipping and pitching. Here, I have drawn my left foot back several inches from the target line.

The square stance is used for the middle irons, long irons, and woods.

The closed stance enables you to take a bigger turn away from the ball, as the right foot is drawn back. This stance is not recommended.

You will find it more to your advantage to use the square and the open stances and forget the closed.

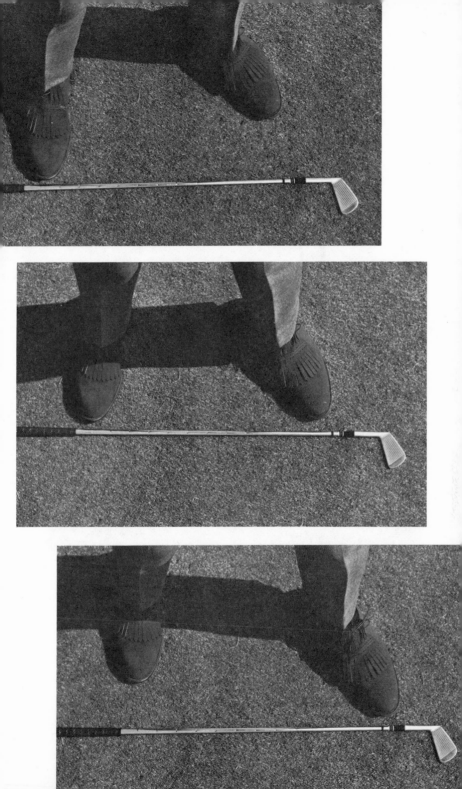

11 POSTURE IS THE SECRET

GOOD POSTURE is one of the secrets of good golf. This is where the swing begins.

Let's start with the feet and legs. Stand in front of a mirror and see how you look.

In the first picture, notice how my knees are pointed in slightly. The weight on the feet is distributed from the balls of the feet to the heels and on the *inside* of the feet. *Never* place your weight on your toes. You will notice in both pictures that I am not on my toes.

In the second picture, see how my knees are flexed. The calves of my legs are straight up. I'm not leaning forward or backward from the ankles.

12 LOOK IN THE MIRROR

LOOK AT THE REST of your posture in the mirror. Your feet are properly placed. The weight is on the inside and distributed from the balls of your feet to the heels.

The knees are flexed slightly and your weight is directly over your feet. You should have the feeling you are starting to sit down, straight down. Notice how my back is straight. I'm not stoop-shouldered or leaning over at the waist.

I have established a square stance. My left foot is pointing out and my right foot is square. The toes of both feet are in line with the target.

Extend your arms down over the imaginary ball. It should be a natural, relaxed feeling. If you reach too far you will have too much weight on your toes. If you are standing too close to the ball, you will have a cramped feeling.

13 CHECK YOUR POSTURE AGAIN

WHEN YOU FINALLY put a club in your hands and place the ball in front of you, everything is perfect. Nothing changes. Your feet, knees, shoulders, and arm extension all remain the same.

Most important, the grip always remains the same.

Take time to check yourself in the mirror at home. First, your feet and knees. Second, your arm extension, your back and shoulders. Finally, pick up a club and see if it still feels the same.

If you check your posture often enough, you'll get the feeling of what is proper, so that when you do get on the first tee, you'll be more comfortable and confident.

14 THE ALL-IMPORTANT GRIP

THE GRIP is the most important part of the golf swing. A good, firm grip will allow you to execute other fundamentals properly.

You should always start with the left hand. You will notice in the first picture how I can hold the club firmly with the last three fingers. This is as it should be.

The end of the club rests under the heel of the hand, and goes diagonally across the first knuckle of the forefinger.

When you clasp your hand on the club, as in the second picture, the thumb is placed on the inside of the shaft—not on top. The reason for placing the thumb on the inside is for a firmer grip. On top, there may be more of a tendency to have the club slip.

You should also know that the "V" formed by the thumb and hand should be pointing directly at your right shoulder when you place the club on the ground.

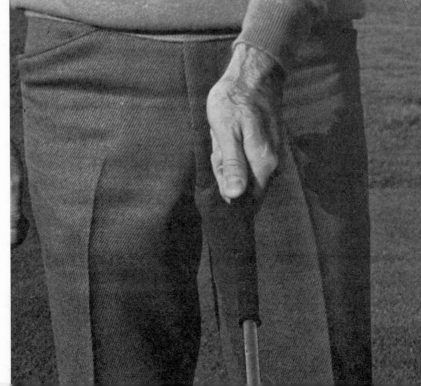

15 TRY OVERLAPPING

THE BEST GRIP for the average person is the overlapping grip. This is formed when you place your right hand on the club and put the little finger of your right hand in between the first and second fingers of your left hand. This, too, helps you establish a firmer overall grip.

Look closely at the fingers of the right hand in the first picture. You can see how I am holding the club in my fingers. The club *never* should be held in the palm of the hands.

Once again, the thumb of the right hand is extended across and on the inside of the shaft. The pressure of the right hand should be carried mostly by the middle two fingers.

Both hands must work together in the golf swing, and you will notice in the third picture that the "V's" formed by both thumbs are pointing directly at the right shoulder. Stand in front of a mirror and look at the grip. Are the "V's" pointing to the right shoulder?

When you first grip the club properly, it will feel uncomfortable. It is different, but after a few weeks it will feel natural.

36

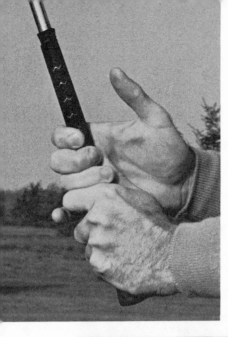

16 TEST THEM ALL

TWO OTHER TYPES of grips are used—the interlocking, shown in the first picture, and the baseball, shown in the second. Everything is basically the same in all three grips, but the interlocking is formed by "locking" the right little finger under and around the left forefinger, as in the first picture. This can help those who have small hands.

When you are practicing, try both grips, the overlapping and the interlocking. See which gives you the best control of the club, and stay with it.

As for the baseball grip, this should only be used as a last resort. You grip the club in the same manner as you did in the other two methods, but the hands are not "tied" together with the fingers.

In all cases, the grip should be firm but not tight.

17 STEP INTO THE SHOT

LINING UP THE GOLF SHOT is as important as the swing itself. There is a proper way to do it, and you should do it the same way every time.

First, you should always walk into the ball with the right foot. Plant your foot where you feel it should be for your stance. Next, place the clubhead behind the ball, as I have done in the first picture. Look up to see where you want to hit the ball, and make certain the clubface is square to the target.

You complete the stance by moving your left foot into its proper position. Now adjust yourself by taking what we call a waggle. If you feel you are too close to the ball, move back slightly. You should feel comfortable over the ball.

When you waggle, move your feet slightly to make certain you have good balance and firm footing. Your grip should be established, although it isn't necessary to hold the club as firmly as you would during the swing. Never take your hands off the club, though.

Look up and double check to be sure you still are lined up

with the target. If it doesn't feel or look right, back away and start over again. Never try to swing if you don't have a comfortable stance.

Once you are set, pause for two or maybe three seconds before you start taking the clubhead back. Otherwise you will be swinging too fast. Most important, use the same approach for all shots. This repetition helps the tempo and rhythm of the entire golf swing.

18 FIND THE BALL

LET'S TAKE A CLOSER LOOK at where you should position the golf ball with the woods at address.

As you can see, I have a square stance. The toes of my shoes are touching the club, which is pointing toward the target. I have placed another club at right angles. One end touches the inside of my left heel. The ball is placed at the other end.

As we move along through the instructions, you now will know exactly what I mean when I refer to the *square* stance and what I mean when I say the ball is positioned off the inside of the left heel.

This is where the ball should be for all shots with the woods, either on the tee or on the fairway. This also is where you should position it for the long irons. However, when I play the middle and short irons I move the ball back about two inches toward the center of the stance. That's all.

19 THE BIG SWING

NOW THAT YOU HAVE A FIRM GRIP established and your stance set, let's talk about the big swing. It's the tee shot with the driver. I'm going to break it into two parts, beginning with the backswing and following with the downswing.

The key to starting the smooth backswing is taking the club-head back low and slow. Never pick the club up and away from the ball. Keep it low to the ground.

The wrist cock begins when the club and left arm are parallel to the ground. With the left arm extended, it comes naturally.

This movement is perfected by making certain the left arm, left shoulder, and left knee act as a one-piece unit. This forces the left knee to turn slightly in toward the right knee.

At address, your weight generally is evenly divided on the inside of your two feet. As you start the backswing, the weight begins its transfer to the inside of the right foot.

At the top of the backswing (third picture) notice how my back is almost facing the target. My left shoulder is underneath my chin. That's a good full shoulder turn.

When you reach the top of the swing, the club never should go past parallel to the ground. Now, most of the weight is on the right side. You may lift your left heel slightly on the backswing, but I suggest you try to keep the heel planted as firmly as possible.

20 "SLIDE" INTO THE BALL

THE DOWNSWING is also started by the left side. You pull down hard with the left arm, keeping it as straight as possible, as I am doing in the first picture. At the same time, keep the right elbow in close to the body.

As soon as you begin the downswing, you also start transferring your weight back to the left side. You do this by planting the left foot firmly.

You also will notice in the first picture how I have started to push off with the inside of the right foot. This not only supplies power, but also helps to move your legs and hips laterally into the hitting area.

It is almost like sliding into the ball.

At impact, as in the second picture, my right elbow is in tight against my body. The left side is straight and firm. But at this point the left side is starting to move out of the way, because I'm still pushing off my right foot. The right side now actually is pushing the left side out of the way, through the hitting area.

Most important, my head is down with my eyes on the ball. You follow through with a nice high finish. The belt buckle or mid-section is facing directly at the target. You can see that in the third picture.

21 | CHIPPING OFF THE STROKES

THE PLAYER WHO CAN CHIP WELL will score well. This is a delicate shot from near the green. You want to chip the ball near the hole, so that you will only need one putt.

You start by using the same grip you use for the other clubs. Choke the club down near the end of the grip, as I'm doing in the picture. *Never* hold the club on the very end for chipping.

The feet are close together. It is a wide-open stance. See how far back I have dropped the left foot. I'm almost facing the hole.

The chip is a low shot. You want the ball to carry onto the green and then run from there. The more you can get the ball to run like a putt once it is on the green, the better off you will be. If you can carry the ball onto the green for the first bounce, it will be to your advantage. You can be more certain of a good bounce. If you bounce it off the fringe, the ball might hit a hole and either stop or take a bad bounce.

Normally I use a No. 5 iron for chipping. However, if it is a short chip, I might use a six or seven iron. When chipping

uphill, use a club with little loft, such as a four or five iron. When chipping downhill, use one with more loft, such as a seven or eight iron, so that you can stop the ball quicker.

Practice this shot. It will help your score.

22 CHOKE DOWN ON CHIPS

LET'S TAKE A CLOSER LOOK at chip shots.

Most important, remember to choke down on the club.

Play the ball back in your stance, off your right heel. Keep your hands *ahead* of the ball at address and throughout the swing. You can see in the first picture how my hands are out in front of the ball.

Chipping is an arm and shoulder movement. There is hardly any wrist action whatsoever. If you study the four pictures, you can see I hardly break my wrists at all. They remain almost stiff.

You must remain still throughout the shot. Your weight is on the left side. Your head must remain down and on the ball. There is no hip or leg turn at all, as you can see.

Take the clubhead back low and slow. You follow through low, too.

The left arm and hand control the whole shot. The back of the left hand always should point toward the hole all the way through the shot, even on the follow through.

Again, keep your hands ahead of the ball. Otherwise you will have a tendency to top the shot or hit behind the ball.

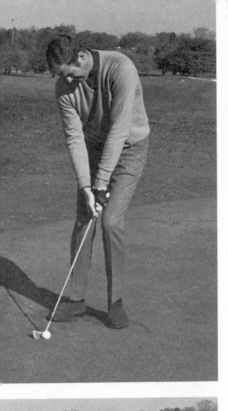

23 AND NOW PITCHING

WHAT IS THE DIFFERENCE between a chip and a pitch? A chip is a low shot that runs on the green toward the hole. A pitch is a high shot that runs little.

You use the pitch on shots from ten to forty yards from the hole. You also use it when you have to pitch the ball over a bunker or water or some other form of trouble in order to get onto the green. The nine iron and wedge are used for this shot.

You choke the club about half way down the grip. The stance still is narrow. Notice how I have brought my left foot up closer to the line of the shot. It only is drawn back about three inches. The stance is not nearly as open as it is for the chip.

The position of the ball at address is moved up slightly, more toward the center of the stance. The weight is on the left side.

For the chip, it is important to keep the hands *ahead* of the ball. But on the pitch shot you position the hands *even* with the ball.

24 THE PITCHING WEDGE

THE PITCH IS A RESTRICTED SWING, because you are not trying to hit the ball far. You are striving for accuracy, not distance.

You take the club back according to how far you must hit the ball. In these pictures I must clear the water. Therefore, I take a three-quarter swing, which is about the most you ever have for this shot.

Notice in the second picture how there is not too much turning with my legs, just the arm and shoulders. The stance is open slightly, with the left foot back about three inches. That permits a good follow-through. There is no restriction or blocking by the left side.

The shot starts by taking the clubhead back slow and easy. The head is down and eyes *always* on the ball. When you come through the shot, you play it straight through, toward the target. Let the left arm and hand control the shot.

At the finish, on this shot, I'm looking right at the hole, as you can see in the fourth picture.

If you only have to pitch the ball a short distance, you will not take as large a swing as illustrated here. This swing in the pictures is for a shot of from fifty to ninety yards. Experience will tell you how large a swing you must take.

25 THE SHORT IRONS

MOVING BACK DOWN THE FAIRWAY, we come into the range
of the short irons, the numbers seven, eight, and nine. With
them you will produce shots that have some of the same delicate characteristics of the pitch. You will also begin to use
a little more power.

These are clubs that will give you high shots. Normally you
will get little roll on the ball once it lands on the green. Therefore it is important to hit the ball right up at the cup.

Accuracy is of prime importance. While you will be shoot-
ing for the greens with the longer irons, you should aim for
the flagstick and try to pinpoint your shots with these clubs.

You now begin to use the principles of the big swing. The
stance is square, although not too wide. Most of the weight
is on the left side, mainly on the inside of the left foot. The
ball is positioned in the front half of your stance, about mid-
way between the left heel and the middle of the stance. Make
certain you still have the good, firm grip. Take a nice, easy
swing. Don't try to kill the ball. Stay down on the ball and
let the club do the work.

Look at the pictures. You can see in the second one, at the
top of the backswing, how the left side (shoulder and leg)
have turned into the ball. The weight has been shifted to the
right side.

The weight is back on the firm left side at impact in the
third picture. The right elbow is in tight to my body. I'm
pushing off my right foot.

Finally, the nice high finish has all the weight on the left.

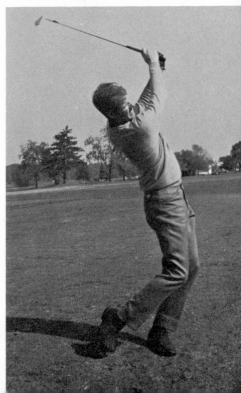

26 THE MIDDLE IRONS

WHEN WE TALK OF THE MIDDLE IRONS, we mean the four, five, and six.

Once again, little has changed. The grip, as always, is the same. The stance is square, although it begins to widen slightly over what you used for the short irons. The position of the golf ball at address still is in the front portion of your stance, just a little back from your left heel.

Remember what I told you about posture? The flex of the knees, the straight back, and the feeling of sitting straight down?

All of this is the same for shots with the driver through the short irons. You can see that in these pictures where I'm using a five iron. However, since the shafts are shorter in the middle and short irons than they are in the woods, it becomes necessary to move closer to the ball.

You never should reach out for the ball. Let your arms hang down naturally, so that you have the same feeling at address. If you do this, you will find that the same swing can be used for all the clubs. You merely have to adjust the length of the backswing according to how far you want to hit the ball.

Whatever you do, don't try to get more from a club than you can. For example, instead of trying to hit a hard five iron, use a four iron and take your nice, easy swing.

27 THE LONG IRONS

Now WE ARE STARTING into the power alley with the long irons, the numbers one, two, and three.

First of all, you should forget about the one iron for now. It is too difficult to use. Even the two iron may be hard for you, but the three iron can be a valuable club.

Since we need more power now, the stance becomes a little wider. You always widen your stance by moving out the right foot. The left foot remains the same for all the shots, because you position the ball in nearly the same spot. For the woods and long irons, the ball should be in line with the inside of the left heel.

You are getting closer to the full swing, so your body turn is more than it was for the middle irons.

Look closely at these three photographs showing good position through the hitting area. With the long irons, it is more of a sweeping-type swing. You brush the ball off the ground.

In the first picture my right elbow is in tight and the left arm firm. I'm starting to push off the inside of the right foot.

At impact, most of the weight is on the left leg. The elbows are in tight.

Finally, the ball is well on its way, but I still have my eyes on the spot where the ball was. Always remember to stay down on the ball. Whatever you do, don't peek. When you finish the follow-through, you'll see the ball flying down the middle.

28 THE FAIRWAY WOODS

THERE ARE SEVERAL IMPORTANT THINGS to remember for the successful use of the fairway woods, numbers two, three, and four.

The stance is slightly wider than it was for the irons. A good indicator is to have the stance here as wide as your shoulders. No more than that, though.

Checking the photographs, you'll notice the slight slope to my shoulders, with the right lower than the left.

The ball, again, is positioned off the inside of the left heel. Starting with the top of the left shoulder, can you see how the stiff left arm and the shaft of the club almost form a straight line to the ball?

Like the long iron, this is a sweeping-type swing. This is evident in the second picture, as I take the clubhead back low and slow.

The key points in the third picture are the shoulder turn (the back is now facing the target); the right hip, which is drawn back; the left knee, which is turned in toward the ball; and the slight lifting of the left heel. What you can't see here is the slight pause at the top of the backswing.

Just before impact in the final picture, you can see how I am bringing the clubhead low into the ball for the sweeping-type hit. Also, I'm driving hard off the right foot and have the left foot firmly planted. The weight now is moving rapidly to the left side. This will result in a good, solid hit.

29 THE ROUGH'S TOUGH

THE ROUGH IS AN IMPORTANT PART of the golf course. Unfortunately, all of us occasionally will hit golf balls in there, but it isn't cause for alarm.

Look at the ball closely to see how deeply it has settled in the long grass. Generally speaking, if you can see two thirds of the ball, as in the top picture, you can use a fairway wood. If you only can see one half or less of the ball, use an iron.

Never take chances from the rough unless the ball is sitting up where you can get the club well into the ball. It is much better to sacrifice distance in order to get the ball back onto the fairway.

Frequently, golfers will attempt to hit the ball too hard out of the high grass, trying to get extra distance. Instead, the grass will grab the clubhead and the ball with hardly move at all. A stroke has been wasted.

When the ball is down in the grass and you are using an iron, the natural tendency is for the iron to tear through the grass. However, you must hit down on the ball. If you try to sweep the ball, as you do in the fairway, you will not get a good, solid hit.

Remember, use your normal stance, bring the clubhead down into the ball, and follow through completely.

The ball will have a tendency to "fly" out of the high grass. Therefore, if you have a six-iron shot, use a seven iron. You should get the same distance.

30 THE HILLS AND DALES

IT WOULD BE WONDERFUL if every ball would land on a smooth, level surface. This cannot be so. Therefore, we must learn to hit the ball from hillsides, too.

The main thing to remember is that the natural tendency is for the ball to go in the direction of the slope of the hill.

In the photograph you can see that the golf ball is "above" my feet at address. The tendency will be to pull the ball down the hill. It is important to aim slightly to the right of the target to allow for this.

As I take my stance, you will notice that I must choke down on the club. It's at least one-half way down the grip, in this case. That's because the ball is above the level of my feet, and therefore is closer to my hands.

Take a slightly wider stance. Play the ball near the center of your stance. Since you are choking down on the club, it becomes a three-quarter swing. This is also to help you maintain balance.

Remember, aim slightly to the right of the target.

Take a nice, easy swing. When you follow through, keep the clubhead going straight in the direction you were aiming.

31 DON'T FALL OVER

NOW WE HAVE THE SITUATION where you must stand over the ball.

Remember what I just told you. The tendency is for the ball to fly in the direction of the slope. If I stand behind the ball and look toward the target, the hill goes from my left to right. This means the ball naturally will fly to the right. Therefore you must aim slightly to the left to allow for this.

Take a slightly open stance. Your weight is back slightly on the heels to keep you from falling over on your toes. Again position the ball off the middle of the stance.

Since you have to reach for the ball, you grip the club right on the end. As always, the hands are up even with the ball.

Remember, swing slow and easy. It's only a three-quarter swing. Don't try to kill the ball. The ball will fly lower than normal from a lie such as this, and usually a little further—it sort of scoots off the ground.

Aiming slightly to the left of the target, take the clubhead back slow and easy. Stay down on the ball. When you follow through, let the clubhead go straight in the direction you were aiming.

32 FOLLOW THE SLOPE DOWN

You will frequently find yourself having to hit the ball downhill. There are a few basic points to remember to help make it easier.

Take a slightly wider stance than you would on a level fairway. The weight should be on the downhill leg, or, as illustrated in the photograph, the left leg. If you have too narrow a stance in a situation such as this, you will lose your balance.

Position the ball back of center, back toward your right foot. You can see I have it about three quarters of the way back.

Once again, it is a restricted swing, about three-quarters. Most important, do not raise up. If you do, you will top the shot. Stay down on the ball. Let the clubhead follow the slope of the hill, straight down. Golfers usually try to pick the ball off the ground, believing they must do this in order to get it in the air. This isn't so.

As for club selection, use less club because the ball will go farther. If it is a normal five-iron shot, use a six iron. Going downhill, it will take a little of the loft off the club.

33 FOLLOW THE SLOPE UP

BALANCE IS VERY IMPORTANT in all golf shots, and especially when you have to hit from unusual positions.

In the case now illustrated, we have to hit the ball uphill. First, take a slightly wider stance. Most of the weight will be on the downhill leg. Position the ball forward in your stance. Choke down slightly on the grip.

Since you are hitting uphill, the ball will get up in the air much faster. This means you must use more club in order to get the needed distance. For example, if I normally would hit a five iron for the required distance, I use a four iron from this position.

This is a restricted swing, too, so that I can maintain good balance. On the follow-through, let the clubhead go right up the hill, in the direction of the target.

Nice and easy, now.

34 THE GOOD SAND LIE

THE PATCHES OF SAND you find on nearly every course can appear as large as a desert when you are stuck in the middle of one. But if you know a few basic principles of bunker play —and practice them—there is no need to fear the piles of sand. One club you should have is a sand wedge. It will make the job easier.

Let's talk first about the good sand lie, where the ball is sitting on top of the sand. Then we'll discuss the buried lie.

When you step into a bunker, determine your address position. You will be hitting about two inches behind the ball.

Plant your feet firmly by wiggling them down in the sand. Besides giving you firm footing, you also can determine the texture of the sand—soft, coarse, loose, wet.

The ball should be positioned near the middle of your stance. Open the stance approximately forty-five degrees to the left of target. That is, pull your left foot well back, as you can see in the picture.

Lay the clubface back so that it is almost flat. Make certain you don't let the clubhead touch the sand. That's a two-stroke penalty.

The scoring—or lines—on the clubface will determine the direction the ball will fly. The ball will pop off the clubface at a right angle to the scoring lines.

35 THE SAND WILL HELP YOU

NOW THAT YOU ARE PROPERLY set up to the ball, let's take a look at the swing.

Choke down on the grip a couple of inches.

Study the series of pictures. You can see there is not much body turn. This is because the stance is so open, with the left foot drawn well back. The knees are flexed. Notice in the first picture how my left arm and the club shaft practically form a straight line to the ball.

Take the clubhead back slow, but more upright. This is because you must come down about two inches behind the ball. It is not a sweeping-type swing as with other clubs. The sand will force the ball out of the trap.

Always lead with your left hand, all the way through the shot. The action feels as if you are slapping the sand, hitting about two inches behind the ball. Make certain you have a strong follow-through. Most people make the mistake of hitting the ball and stopping. You *must* follow through.

You learn from practice how much sand to take. But to a certain extent, you can determine this when you are planting your feet. If it is easy to dig in with your feet and they sink quickly, then the sand is soft. This means the club will cut into the sand easily and you should take slightly more sand. If you find it hard to plant your feet, then the sand is coarse or wet. The club will bounce through it more and you will not be able to take as much.

36 THE BURIED SAND LIE

LOOK AT THE WAY this golf ball is buried in the sand. As they say, if you hit it in there, you have to play it out. You have to play this shot differently than a good sand lie.

First of all, anchor your feet the same way and use the open stance, with the left foot drawn well back from the target line.

However, now you must play the ball *back* in your stance. It almost is in line with the inside of the right foot.

Look at the clubhead on the sand wedge. Do you notice how the blade is slightly more squared than it is for the good sand lie? This is because you cannot slap the ball out of there. You must dig it out.

Again, choke up slightly on the grip. Observe that my hands are slightly ahead of the ball at address. This is as it should be. They should be in that position when you dig the ball out, too.

As a reminder, never touch the sand with your club. This is called "grounding." If you do, it will cost you two penalty strokes. You can see how I'm holding the club about one inch above the sand.

37 DIG THE BALL OUT

Now, LET'S POP THE GOLF BALL out of its buried lie in the sand and onto the green.

Your feet are firmly planted. The knees are flexed—as they are for all shots. The stance is open.

Remember, instead of a low, sweeping backswing, you pick the clubhead up sooner. There is very little leg movement. It mostly is arm and shoulders.

Coming back into the ball, always lead with the left arm and hand. Notice how I have the left arm extended in the second picture. The left arm pulls the club through the shot, with the left hand leading the way. The back of the left hand always is going toward the target.

You should hit the sand about two inches behind the ball. Because the ball is buried, you have to dig under it. Let this be the normal arc of the swing. Don't try to steer the ball out or gouge it out.

Complete success will depend on the follow-through. This you must do on all sand shots. Force yourself to do it, and make it all part of the swing. Too many people hit the ball, hesitate, and then follow through. The result is that they only move the ball a few feet.

This is a shot that needs practice.

38 EVERYONE NEEDS PRACTICE

THERE IS MORE TO GOLF than going out and playing nine or eighteen holes. If you want to play well, you must find time to practice. This is the time to work on your game, especially the weak points.

Begin with the wedge and work back through the clubs. Concentrate on the short irons, along with pitching and chipping. You can do this in your own backyard.

You must learn to use all the clubs, so practice with them all, not just your favorites. Try to develop as smooth a swing as possible.

You can find out your own capabilities in practice. See how far you can hit the ball with control, then concentrate on the swing that will give you control.

Don't try to slam the ball as hard as you can every time. Experiment. Go to the practice tee with a plan in mind. Know what you want to accomplish on that particular day.

If you have a chance, practice a little just after you have finished playing a round. At that time you clearly remember where you had the trouble and you can work on those shots.

If you can do the fundamentals and do them right, over and over again, you will be a fine golfer.

39 KEEP YOUR CLUBS SHINING

BE PROUD OF YOUR GOLF EQUIPMENT and keep your clubs and the bag as clean as possible. There is a proper place to store everything at home. Put your clubs there, instead of throwing them on the garage floor.

After you have finished for the day, take a bristle scrub brush and clean the faces of your clubs. Do not use a wire brush or steel wool. A little furniture polish on the tops of your woods will keep them shining.

Carry a towel with you when you play. Make this part of your equipment. You can use it to clean your golf ball and to keep the club faces clean and dry at all times. You would be surprised how much a little dirt in the grooves of the club-face can affect the flight of the ball.

If you can't get the dirt out with the towel, take the pointed end of a tee and run it through the grooves.

It is wise to have covers for your woods to protect them from getting nicked or scarred from the irons bouncing around in the bag. Some people even like to have a cover for their putter for the same reason.

Your golf shoes are part of the equipment, too. Keep them polished and clean. In fact, be generally neat and clean in your appearance on the golf course.

40 KNOW THE RULES

THE OFFICIAL RULES OF GOLF are for everyone, not only the young players such as yourself, but for the leading professionals as well.

Always remember one thing: The Rules of Golf are made to help you. That is why you should take time to know at least the basic rules, and should play by these rules.

The United States Golf Association is the governing body of golf in this country. It always has made certain that the rules are fair and equal for all golfers, regardless of their ability.

One of the most important things to remember under the rules is to be honest with yourself and your friends. Always mark down your right score, especially if you are in competition.

You can obtain a copy of the rules from the United States Golf Association, Golf House, 40 East 38th Street, New York, New York 10016.

EPILOGUE: The Game of a Lifetime

NOW THAT YOU HAVE READ THIS BOOK, you should be well on your way to more enjoyable golf—even if you are not quite ready to join the professional tour.

One of the wonderful features of this game is that you can play it for many years. There is no age limit to golf. For many people, golf is their prime source of recreation long after they have gone into retirement.

The electric golf carts make it possible for older people to continue playing long after they find it difficult to walk any distance.

When the weather is pleasant and you are with friends, there isn't a finer way to spend a few hours.

Sure, we all know this can be a frustrating game, but you are on the course to have fun. Practice what I've told you and you will be able to play well enough to enjoy it for the rest of your years.

Maybe someday, somewhere, we'll meet on the first tee. I hope so.

Play well.